Whispers from Her Husband's Heart

*they began with the rosebud
and ended with my kiss*

Whispers from Her Husband's Heart

they began with the rosebud
and ended with my kiss

BRIAN

Library of Congress Control Number:		2016902206
ISBN:	Hardcover	978-1-5144-5872-3
	Softcover	978-1-5144-5871-6
	eBook	978-1-5144-5870-9

Cover Art by Hannah B.

Print information available on the last page.

Rev. date: 03/17/2016

100% of profits realized from this book will be donated to A Sanctuary At Discovery Bay, a 501c3 not for profit organization dedicated to disabled American veterans.

To order additional copies of this book, contact:
Xlibris
1-888-795-4274
www.Xlibris.com
Orders@Xlibris.com
735587

Foreword

This is all for you, Jo
Thanks be to God.

Whispers is an extended love story to my wife, Jo, covering the eighteen or so years my life was blessed with her presence. My pastor once told me that the day I married Jo was the luckiest day of my life. I told him that I certainly knew that and that on that day it became my calling to be sure it was the luckiest day in hers! We both approached our marriage in such a way. I proposed to Jo in the Fall of 1997. Jo and I were living in Saint Louis, MO., and I had spent a week with my mother in Dallas/Fort Worth who was suffering discomfort from a minor illness. When she recovered, I telephoned Jo in Saint Louis and asked her to meet me the next day when I flew from Dallas in her red and white ski sweater. She agreed to do so, and upon departure from Dallas, I stopped by the airport florist and ordered a dozen red rosebuds, as the plane grew nearer Saint Louis, I took eleven of those rosebud and gave one to the first eleven people getting off the plane. I asked them to look for a pretty blonde lady in a red ski sweater as they deplaned. They were to hand the rosebud to that lady and tell her the rosebud was from Brian. I deplaned with the twelfth rosebud and proposed to Jo. She cried, but thankfully said yes.

What a grand experience!!

This book is formatted in an unusual manner. After each quatrain, there is an unnumbered, blank page. As you read the quatrains and experience the love that they depict, I encourage you to write your own thoughts about that most important person in your life. You owe it to them.

I had planned a book of two sections, but Jo unexpectedly passed away, and I needed to add a third and fourth. A close friend said, "Brian, you really loved her." I replied, "yes, I did and I still do!" There were tear stains on the manuscript as I wrote this foreword. They were tears borne of love and joy.

Thanks be to God!

Love, Brian

whispers from her husband's heart

Brian

Table of Contents

She Is A Garden of Delight

Brian

In the garden where I'm living,
there are beautiful new blooms,
Now I know that I'm forgiven,
for God's newest blessing looms.

She's everything that love can give,
she's a bloom extraordinaire.
She makes my time a life to live,
when she brings life's freshest air.

She's my life's possibilities,
bringing all the things I might.
The soft caressing of her breeze,
she's a garden of delight.

The Silence of Our Breeze

Brian

Within the silence of our breeze,
is a story yet untold.
Yet in its telling are the keys,
our love as pure as gold.

We have just begun the telling,
of the things to be our life.
The dream that's to be our dwelling,
the day she became my wife.

Yes, it's a story yet untold,
with an ending sure to please.
The faith and love that's purest gold,
the true silence of our breeze.

We're Going Fishing For Our Dreams

Brian

The dreams we had begun to share,
were beginning to be real.
When we cast lines for whom we cared,
what we really hoped to feel.

There can be no guaranteeing,
when you try to fish for dreams,
Casting, casting, then repeating,
is the way to go it seems.

We search for everything that gleams,
so that we can always know,
We're going fishing for our dreams,
that's the place we want to go.

The Sweetest Little Heart

Brian

She is the sweetest little heart,
to come into my life.
Came to give my heart a start,
and so became my wife.

Every moment of her day,
is there to serve another.
She always seems to find a way,
to go a little further.

If all of us were more like her,
the world would be ideal.
The joy that we would all prefer,
makes paradise surreal.

There Are Some Rainbows in Her Eyes

Brian

I saw rainbows in our future,
there were rainbows on my mind.
Everything that I could give her,
gifts for her that I might find.

When I searched the world over,
nowhere else on earth could be,
nowhere else could I discover,
one so wonderful as she.

When I recognized my duty,
for the things she brought to me,
when I can see in her beauty,
rainbows in her eyes for me.

A Touch in Our Afternoon

Brian

We both live in our sunset years,
a bit like our afternoon,
We realize our sundown nears,
our good times will end too soon.

No one can know the joy we feel,
fate bestows another chance.
We can't believe it's really real,
that we have another dance.

Our sunset years will be our best,
no other time can compare.
She's much sweeter than all the rest,
an afternoon's touch so rare.

Star Bright, Star Bright

Brian

Hold me close to dance as night falls,
she's the princess of the ball,
She's endearing so delightful,
she's the brightest star of all.

What I did to get that blessing,
I don't think I'll ever know.
My good fortune keeps me guessing,
why she seems to love me so.

It's no accident that blessing,
didn't come from someone near,
After my sincere confessing,
he gave me a treasure dear.

A River of Lights

Brian

As the evening grew colder,
we saw a river of lights.
Her head rested on my shoulder,
that most beautiful of nights.

Not only her beauty but her peace,
were with me that dearest night.
That cold dark night had pain's release,
as we viewed the starry light.

I found my fingers in her hair,
when held her hand in mine.
Then when our blanket warmed with care,
I knew she was really mine.

Sailing Alone

Brian

Her light reflected on the water,
as we stood beside the lake.
We spoke of all that mattered,
the directions we might take.

We shared portraits of our partings,
from the lives we used to live.
With the pain of souls still smarting,
there was nothing left to give.

Sailing alone in empty space,
she reached out and touched my hand.
She gave my lonely heart a taste,
at love she might still command.

My Trilling Nachtigall

Brian

Where can sweet sorrow really go,
when your heart is torn in two?
When all the things you'd hope to know,
and there's nothing left for you?

Sweet sounds from outside come to me,
they give my lonely heart a thrill.
That little bird, high in the tree,
sweetly sings her haunting trill.

She is the girl I hold so dear,
lonely nights are I can't recall.
Her songs are safe within my ear,
she is my trilling nachtigall.

Les Peintures Blanc

Brian

The tableaux we had painted,
were as blank as they could be.
Both the brushes used were tainted,
the pictures weren't you and me.

Pictures of two live's both failing,
sad and lonely were the norm,
Two lives off their tracks derailing,
wanting to once more perform.

Then one day we met together,
in a meeting left to chance.
Turned our backs on stormy weather,
chose a beautiful romance.

Golden Tapestry

Brian

The tapestry we are weaving,
has a tender, golden edge.
We are staring unbelieving,
at the love we hope to pledge.

Nothing else has come before us,
nowhere near a love like this.
that love has come to adore us,
like it did when we first kissed.

Love that we can give each other,
unrestricted, knows no bounds.
Tender touch we give as lovers,
bells ringing with sweet, pure sounds.

Ripening Corn and Summer's Rain

Brian

Ripening corn and summer's rain,
harbingers of tomorrow.
We take a chance with love again,
a life bereft of sorrow.

Just as corn grows ever stronger,
as it strains toward the light,
our romance will be here longer,
like the corn, we'll be alright.

Like corn our love began in spring,
and we watched it slowly grow,
With all the wonders it could bring,
and the gifts it would bestow.

Our Imaginary Place

Brian

It's what every couple longs for,
an imaginary place,
a secret place without a door,
it's where both of us are safe.

The secret place that isn't real,
it exists within our minds.
But it's a place we both can feel,
it's where love begins to bind.

It's there with us every day,
never something to conceal.
All cuddled in the things we say,
we both know that place is real.

Every Day Is a Dance For Her

Brian

She greets all her days with a smile,
bringing hours of peaceful bliss.
Singing sweetly for a while,
harmony you shouldn't miss.

She loves the simple things of life,
always says not me, but you.
She only wants to be my wife,
It's her sweet spirit so true

Her sweet touches cause me to purr,
as we waltz around our room.
Every day is a dance for her,
and I want to waltz there, too.

When Does a Heart Need Love's Repair?

Brian

When a pair is somehow ruptured,
and you're suddenly alone,
your heart is fair to be captured,
no more living just as one.

When you see the one you're meeting,
and you know that she's the one,
best think hard about your greeting,
less you lose the chance you've won.

When does a heart need love's repair?
that's a question you must ask.
The day your sweetheart meets you there,
with the love you sought at last.

She Is The Lady of My Lake

Brian

Where all life's rivers join to make,
and two lovers come to meet.
Here lives the lady of my lake.
She's my lady, oh so sweet.

No one can know how wonderful,
is the love she brings to me,
She makes our life so beautiful,
there it is for all to see.

Every day she greets me beaming,
as I from a dream awake.
She gives life a special meaning,
she's the lady of my lake.

The Wisdom From Above

Brian

A smile that causes sun to shine,
always lurks around her lips.
When her eyes look deep into mine,
then she can find my fingertips.

The simple joy those acts can bring,
bind us tight so we are one.
And then we hope there's not a thing,
that either of us haven't done.

Hand in hand when we kneel to pray,
we feel the beauty of our love.
We want to know what God would say,
in his wisdom from above.

While I'm Gone

Brian

There is no love that man can make,
that equals what I give to you.
I give with every breath I take,
all the love you give me, too.

I see your face and lovely smile,
each time I pause and close my eyes.
And thinking back a little while,
how wonderful my sweet surprise.

I'll just be gone a little while,
your name is always in my heart.
Just watch for me, and bring your smile,
can't stand the times when we are apart.

The Bliss That Is Ours

Brian

All the dreams of bliss we promised,
and fell helplessly in love,
then the loving that God gave us,
was a blessing from above.

His blessed goal is in our hand,
at the place where we must go.
The holy rings, our wedding bands,
there's the truth we need to know.

We won't know what price were paying,
but our chins are held up high.
Hold each other's hand while praying,
long before we say goodbye.

Her Warrior Magician

Brian

Warrior's magic strength he gives her,
cut from the forest's strongest tree.
Care for her is always better,
always faithful, always free.

A simple lesson he had learned,
what you give is what you get.
Not a thing you think you're earning,
Lesson he should not forget.

Every gift in life and love,
have been paid for by His grace.
they're created high above,
a result of Gods embrace.

She Loves The Pink and White Petunias

Brian

She loved the pink and white petunias,
very quickly, I did too.
They created love between us,
gave our hearts a thing to do.

When the pinks were early blooming,
with the petals in the spring.
Every day she's snipping, pruning,
really made our love take wing.

We were watching our love growing,
from the stems and leaves it came.
With the love we shared bestowing,
they left a beautiful name.

She Loved Me Anyway

Brian

———————————————————————————————•

A stranger in a stranger's land,
is the man I was that day.
I lived a life on sifting sand,
but she loved me anyway.

There can't be a valid reason,
that she opened up to me.
For sure I'm not all that pleasing,
there that everyone can see.

Trying my best to impress her,
going far out of my way.
I was not the ideal treasure,
but she loved me anyway.

I'm Dancing With a Star

Brian

We never know what fortune brings,
we can only breathe a sigh,
When listening how the angels sing,
then we know that God is nigh.

The pretty lady on my arm,
is dancing along with me,
I'm floored completely by her charm,
no one's pure and good as she.

The wonderful things that could be,
never thought I'd come this far.
A gift that God has made for me,
now I'm dancing with a star.

All Our Steps Beyond This Moment

Brian

We've been given second chances,
in our early years of life.
Some defeats and some advances,
now's the time to end the strife.

As we search so long for answers,
time is really nature's gift.
Now we are the leading dancers,
it's the burden we must lift.

It's our choice to not be dormant,
and be what we want to be,
All our steps beyond this moment,
makes us what we ought to be.

Angel By My Side

Brian

When she wakes and softly greets me,
cuddled safely in her dreams,
fresh from sleeping, oh so deeply,
angel by my side she seems.

When I touch her cheek so sweetly,
stroke her brow so soft and fine,
angel that I love completely,
can't believe she's really mine.

When she wakes and softly greets me,
letting go the passing dream,
hand in hand her love completes me.
angel by my side she seems.

Flowers of Our Night

Brian

The many flowers of our nights,
have bloomed with fragrant blossom,
Speaking softly of what we might,
passing through the simply awesome.

Thinking we had missed life's party,
left to celebrate alone,
we raised our chins, laughed so hearty,
the party was not yet done,

Celebrations are funny things,
our lives were no exception.
These two old friends danced many rings,
around their world's perception.

Autumn Leaves

Brian

Comes now the colors of the fall,
but now we can't enjoy them,
For only one can't see them all,
as God grandly deploys them.

As leaves let go and slowly fall,
they're dislodged by autumn's breeze.
and float down from trees so tall,
they're awaiting winter's freeze.

Much like them we are doomed to fall,
now the trees are stripped of leaves,
just as the ones left to recall,
those memories left as keys.

Our Love's Afterglow

Brian

In the small hours of the night,
comes a gentle afterglow.
The slowly disappearing light,
is the sadness that I know.

The memory to which I cling,
has the sweetest afterglow.
The melody I'll always sing,
to my sweet departed Jo.

She was the girl that I so loved,
the soul of her afterglow,
the gift who came from high above,
she was my sweet-hearted Jo.

In Her Beauty She walked Away

Brian

In her beauty, walking proudly,
tears of sadness letting go,
night time echoes cry so loudly,
letting go the love I know

No one knows the pain I'm feeling,
people come to comfort me.
They can't know my heart is reeling,
all they know is what they see.

We've just ended life's great story,
hand in hand until the last.
Knowing all of loves great glory,
both our fingers holding fast.

All The Things That Ever Mattered

Brian

When the only thing that matters,
as my life began to twirl,
when that life was left in tatters,
she was this man's precious girl.

I must always look to heaven,
and so hope to find her there.
I'm the man to much was given,
by my lady, oh so fair.

All the things that ever mattered,
all the victories we won,
all our hopes and dreams are scattered,
sadly, half of me is gone.

See Her Again Someday

Brian

Next to God, I see her kneeling
all her troubled battles won,
not with pain will she be dealing,
she's in heaven with His son.

Nothing more for me to whisper,
nothing more for me to say.
Let us all take comfort with her,
her sweet smile will light the day,

She held high a guiding beacon,
lighting darkness on our way.
So that I might have a reason,
to see her again someday.

The Little Ring Upon My Finger

Brian

Resting on my little finger,
is the ring she wore on hers,
When she could no longer linger,
it's the one I now prefer.

That little ring meant all the things,
that we hoped our love to be,
when on her hand I placed that ring,
she gave all of her to me.

That golden ring, always giving,
on my hand it's now defined.
From her hand her love's still giving,
it will be forever mine.

Who Said She Had To Melt Away?

Brian

Who said she had to melt away,
to insist she would depart,
to think that I could ever say,
to remove her from my heart?

If they hadn't paid attention,
to the love we always shared,
wouldn't know of our intentions,
couldn't know how much we cared.

She didn't have to melt away,
it's a thing I truly know.
She's here forever and a day,
for my heart won't let her go.

A Star Began To Shine That Day

Brian

We loved to watch the stars at night,
didn't have too much to say,
just knew that where we were was right,
that God led us on our way.

Those nights full of love and caring,
always ended up in grins.
Those small tidbits of our sharing,
always counted up as wins.

When I could see that starlight ray,
so I could recall her face.
A star began to shine that day,
made our nights a better place.

Fireflies in Our Night

Brian

When there were fireflies in our night,
she would always want to see,
how many more would show their light,
and point them out to me.

Now when the twilight brings our fireflies,
I still always think of Jo.
Then I watch until the sunrise,
and thinking I loved her so.

My tears will never put away,
all her fireflies in my life.
I know we'll meet again someday,
watching fireflies in the night.

Count Each and Every Kiss

Brian

I count each and every kiss.
that had ever touched our hearts.
For fear there's one that I might miss,
on the day that she departs.

The fact that she stood next to me,
as only that woman could,
said there was no pretext to be,
standing by my side she stood.

Those kisses that we always shared,
they still fill my memories.
Reminding me how much we cared,
lips to meet in reveries.

The Land of Forever

Brian

There is no land of forever,
although I wish it so to be,
I could slice through death cold tether,
and could hold her close to me.

When the touch of her hand in mine,
brought me a love I longed to hold,
when she stepped across heavens line,
and I kissed her lips so cold.

Her words of love came back to me,
as her story's last chapter told.
When God came close to set her free,
and showed the beauty of her soul.

When The One You Love Is Leaving

Brian

When the one you love is leaving,
and her home is far away,
then the war I'm not yet winning
is the final price to pay.

She can look down from the highest,
so to keep me safe and free.
Telling me Gods path is wisest,
that he cares for you and me.

Yes, the battles not yet over,
are a burden for my heart.
All my cares are just cover,
all that mattered merely departs.

To Pave Her Way

Brian

Her passing through that gate so stony,
was the saddest day for me.
I realized that it came only,
when God finally set her free.

No more pain and no more sickness,
now her face is wreathed in smiles.
Now she lives with God her witness,
not to see the devil's wiles.

With the sweetest kiss I tendered,
then I sent her on her way,
with my warmest hug to send her,
loving gift to pave her way.

The Greyest Sky and Bittersweet

Brian

The greyest sky and bittersweet,
left at the end of her days.
The day that made her life complete,
then it took her soul away.

Was about to leave for good that day,
the sweetest soul I'd ever known,
the hardest price I'd ever pay,
the sweetness I could never own.

For all that knew her heart so kind,
sweet love from that heart would pour,
with the touch of her hand in mine,
now, never more, never more.

Love For All Eternity

Brian

None could be more appealing,
than my sweetheart was to me.
She brought life's most precious feeling,
love for all eternity.

Brought the finest part of living,
gave a new spark to our home,
She had no restraint on giving,
all her gifts for me alone.

How on earth can I repay her,
give her what she gave to me,
hold back nothing to delay her,
love for all eternity?

Echoes in My Mind

Brian

Now my home resounds with echoes,
of the sounds she used to lend,
of the way we strove to be close,
and the songs her love to send.

The words from deep within my heart,
will be gushing from me still,
as they were from my very start,
to my very end they will.

Echoes come in many a form,
a glance, a smile, or a scent.
Peace that always follows the storm,
with the messages it sends.

Christmas Joy

Brian

However might we remember,
a person we longed to see,
she gave her last December,
Christmas joy for you and me.

Of all the things she did for me,
she would do for me alone,
an evidence for all to see,
her sweet joy and need postponed.

Her Christmas joy infused our home,
it was blessed for all to see,
the benefit by her alone,
that meant everything to me.

Drifting Through Time

Brian

From the first day of our meeting,
on that lucky day we met,
Our good days began repeating,
when our compasses were set.

We had made our best selection,
and entered each other's life.
I was to be her husband,
and she was to be my wife.

While throughout our time we drifted,
lazy drifting hand and hand.
Hazy days when we were gifted,
joined by golden wedding bands.

Her Last Serenade

Brian

She was sunshine on my shoulder,
when I sang that serenade.
Then my heart grew quickly colder,
as my hope began to fade.

She was my beautiful princess,
beyond anything I'd known,
She became my precious songstress,
the flower from seeds we'd sown.

The words were born for her last song,
as we both became afraid,
The thing that we had feared so long,
came with her last serenade.

My Precious Jo

Brian

My precious Jo, my morning star,
her sweet heart was always mine,
I never dreamed I'd come so far,
when I touched her soul so fine,

When God entrusted her to me,
with a life for us to share,
I wondered then at what might be,
with a soul, so sweet, so fair.

She never failed to be with me,
never failing to bestow,
no sweeter love could ever be,
always there, my precious Jo.

Nevermore Will She Be Weeping

Brian

Nevermore will she be weeping,
all her struggles done and gone.
Now she's resting, quietly sleeping,
sadly, now my queen is gone.

I will never find another,
gentle soul as sweet as she,
Nor can I want to discover,
one that meant as much to me.

The love and peace she's always bringing,
gently help the things we do,
with the songs she's always singing,
let's us start our life anew.

Our Smiles Are Not Yet Frowns

Brian

As we began to dance the now,
with a sky so bittersweet,
too soon leaving just to allow,
life's sad story to complete.

No! we spoke as one together,
our life's story isn't done.
This will end as we would rather,
laughing, giggling, having fun.

Even though our laughter's over,
still our smiles are not yet frowns,
tears of grief have yet to cover,
our precious love that had no bounds.

A Husbands Farewell

Brian

Be still my soul, for nigh's the time I leave you,
I go to God in just a little while.
The love we've shared is precious beyond measure,
I'll take with me the sweetness of your smile.

Where e'er you go my heart will be there with you,
My soul will watch to keep you safe and free,
No one can touch the love we've shared together,
because my part, I'm taking home with me.

I'll wait for you beside my Lord and Savior.
I'm safe and loved inside his grace divine.
Be happy dear, you'll never be forgotten,
my life was whole because your heart was mine.

The Crying of My Heart

Brian

If the song you hear me singing,
as you suddenly depart,
has a woeful, painful ringing,
it's the crying of my heart.

No melody can replace you,
you're the finest ever found.
To our love I'll always be true,
and to your heart I'll be bound.

All the time our marriage gave us,
was a gift for me and you.
It's God's tender way to save us,
as we start our life anew.

A La Fin (Our Epitaph)

Brian

They sleep beneath their chosen earth,
Far from the place that gave them birth,
Their gentle ways will always dwell,
In hearts that knew and loved them well.

CPSIA information can be obtained
at www.ICGtesting.com
Printed in the USA
LVHW031444020623
748739LV00031B/1097/J